BASICS OF RUBY PROGRAMMING

DR DHEERAJ MEHROTRA

Made with ♥ on the Notion Press Platform
www.notionpress.com

Contents

PREFACE

Hello, and welcome to the exciting world of Ruby programming! As I approach the point at which I will initiate you into the complicated dance that is code and creativity, I am overcome with both enthusiasm and a tremendous feeling of duty. This book is more than just a collection of programming paradigms and rules of syntax; it is a guided trip through the language that has won the hearts of developers all over the globe.

Ruby is not only a programming language; instead, it is an expression of beauty, simplicity, and delight for software developers. In the following articles, I will do my best to demystify Ruby and make it understandable not just for inexperienced programmers interested in making their first steps into the world of programming but also for more seasoned programmers eager to broaden their range of capabilities.

This journey is about comprehending Ruby's "how" and appreciating Ruby's "why." As we explore various ideas, from the most basic building blocks to the complexities of object-oriented programming, I was hoping you could learn the syntax and embrace the philosophy that makes Ruby a language unlike any other. If you are successful in doing so, I will consider this course a success.

I owe a debt of thanks to the active Ruby community and the inventors of this lovely programming language, whose enthusiasm and ingenuity continue to change the landscape of contemporary programming. Their willingness to share ideas, work together, and never give up in their search for superior solutions is an example and a model for us to follow.

This book was written with you, the reader, in mind. Whether you are a student eager to learn, a professional trying to enhance your abilities, or just a curious mind attracted to the beauty of code, this book was written with you in mind. The exercises, examples, and tales are meant to establish a relationship between you and the language, creating an atmosphere where learning is about the goal and the thrilling trip itself.

As you set out on this journey, I want to encourage you to try new things, to ask questions, and open yourself up to the excitement of discovery. Ruby is more than a tool; it is a travelling partner for your coding journey. You will need a map to explore the enormous geography of Ruby and unleash its potential to bring your ideas to life. May this book serve as that guide for you.

Best of luck with your programming!

Dr Dheeraj Mehrotra

I

Introduction to Ruby

Ruby is a dynamic, object-oriented programming language designed for simplicity and productivity. It has an elegant syntax, is natural to read and is easy to write.

Ruby is often used for web development, scripting, and general-purpose programming.

Installing Ruby:

Before you start programming in Ruby, you must install it on your machine. Follow these steps:

Linux/Mac:

Most Linux distributions come with Ruby pre-installed. You can check by opening a terminal and typing ruby -v.

For macOS, you can use the built-in Ruby or install a version manager like RVM (Ruby Version Manager) or rbenv.

Windows:

Download the RubyInstaller from rubyinstaller.org.

Follow the installation instructions and check the box that adds Ruby to your system path.

Your First Ruby Program:

Once Ruby is installed, create a simple "Hello, World!" program.

hello.rb

puts "Hello, World!"

• 3 •

Save this file with a .rb extension, for example, hello.rb. To run it, open a terminal, navigate to the file's directory, and type:

ruby hello.rb

You should see the output: Hello, World!

Basic Ruby Concepts:

Variables:

Ruby uses dynamic typing. You don't need to declare the variable type; Ruby infers it.

```ruby
name = "John"
age = 25
```

name = "John" age = 25

Data Types:

Ruby supports various data types, such as strings, numbers, arrays, hashes, symbols, etc.

Control Flow:

Use if, else, and elsif for conditional statements.

```ruby
if condition
  # code
elsif another_condition
  # code
else
  # code
end
```

if condition # code elsif another_condition # code else # code end

Loops:

Ruby supports while, until, for, and iterator methods like each.

```ruby
5.times do
  puts "Ruby is fun!"
end
```

5.times do puts "Ruby is fun!" end

Arrays and Hashes:

```ruby
# Array
fruits = ["apple", "banana", "orange"]

# Hash
person = { "name" => "John", "age" => 25 }
```

 # Array fruits = ["apple", "banana", "orange"] # Hash person = { "name" => "John", "age" => 25 }

Methods:

Define methods using the def keyword.

```ruby
def greet(name)
  puts "Hello, #(name)!"
end

greet("Alice")
```

def greet(name) puts "Hello, #{name}!" end greet("Alice")

Object-Oriented Programming (OOP) in Ruby:

Ruby is an object-oriented language, and everything in Ruby is an object.

Classes and Objects:

```ruby
class Dog
  def initialize(name)
    @name = name
  end

  def bark
    puts "Woof, #{@name}!"
  end
end

my_dog = Dog.new("Buddy")
my_dog.bark
```

class Dog def initialize(name) @name = name end def bark puts "Woof, #{@name}!" end end my_dog = Dog.new("Buddy") my_dog.bark

Inheritance:

```ruby
class Labrador < Dog
  def swim
    puts "#{@name} is swimming!"
  end
end


my_labrador = Labrador.new("Max")
my_labrador.bark
my_labrador.swim
```

class Labrador < Dog def swim

puts "#{@name} is swimming!"

end end my_labrador = Labrador.new("Max")

my_labrador.bark my_labrador.swim

File Handling:

Ruby makes file handling simple.

Reading from a File:

rubyCopy code

File.open("example.txt", "r") do |file| puts file.read end

•

Writing to a File:

rubyCopy code

File.open("example.txt", "w") do |file| file.puts "Hello, File!" end

Ruby Gems:

RubyGems is Ruby's package manager. You can use it to install libraries (gems) to extend Ruby's functionality.

gem install gem_name

Conclusion:

This tutorial provides a basic introduction to Ruby programming. There's much more to explore, including web development with Ruby on Rails, testing with RSpec, and more advanced Ruby features. The official Ruby documentation is an excellent resource for further learning.

Happy coding with Ruby!

II
Advantages of RUBY

Ruby, a dynamic, object-oriented programming language, has gained popularity for various reasons. Here are some of the advantages of using Ruby:

Elegant Syntax: Ruby is known for its clean and elegant syntax, focusing on readability and simplicity. This makes it easy for developers to write and maintain code.

Object-Oriented: Ruby is a fully object-oriented language, where everything is an object. This promotes a modular and organized approach to programming.

Dynamic Typing: Ruby is dynamically typed, allowing developers to write code more flexibly. Variable types are determined at runtime, making writing and understanding code easier.

Metaprogramming: Ruby's metaprogramming capabilities allow developers to write code that can modify its structure, enabling powerful and flexible abstractions.

Rails Framework: Ruby on Rails (Rails) is a powerful and developer-friendly web application framework built on Ruby. It follows the convention over configuration (CoC) and don't repeat yourself (DRY) principles, making web development efficient and enjoyable.

Community and Ecosystem: Ruby has a vibrant and supportive community. The RubyGems package manager provides access to a vast ecosystem of libraries and tools, simplifying development tasks.

Productivity: Ruby emphasizes developer happiness and productivity. Its concise syntax and high-level abstractions enable developers to write code quickly and efficiently.

Readability: The language's syntax is designed to be readable and expressive, promoting a natural flow of logic that is easy to understand, even for those new to the language.

Flexibility: Ruby is a flexible language that allows developers to choose their programming paradigm (procedural, functional, or object-oriented) based on the needs of a particular project.

Community-Driven Development: The Ruby community is actively involved in the development of the language. The open-source nature of Ruby allows developers to contribute to its growth and improvement.

Cross-Platform Compatibility: Ruby is cross-platform, meaning that code written in Ruby can run on various operating systems without modification.

Testing Frameworks: Ruby has robust testing frameworks, such as RSpec and MiniTest, which encourage and facilitate test-driven development (TDD).

Scalability: While Ruby is often associated with small to medium-sized projects, it is also used in large-scale applications. When combined with appropriate architectural patterns and tools, Ruby applications can scale effectively.

Community Conventions: Ruby follows community conventions and best practices, making it easier for developers to collaborate on projects and maintain consistency across the codebase.

Active Development: The language continues to evolve with new versions and features, ensuring it remains relevant and competitive in the ever-changing landscape of programming languages.

• • •

These advantages contribute to Ruby's popularity and make it a preferred choice for many developers, particularly in web development and other domains where rapid development and readability are crucial.

III

Applications of RUBY

Ruby is a versatile programming language that finds applications across various domains. Some of the notable applications of Ruby include:

Web Development:

Ruby on Rails (Rails): Ruby is most famous for its web development framework, Ruby on Rails. Rails follows the convention over configuration (CoC) and don't repeat yourself (DRY) principles, making it a powerful and efficient tool for building web applications.

Startups and Prototyping:

Ruby, and particularly Ruby on Rails, is a popular choice for startups due to its quick development cycles. Its elegant syntax allows developers to prototype and build MVPs (Minimum Viable Products) rapidly.

Automation and Scripting:

Ruby's concise and readable syntax makes it suitable for automation scripts. It is often used for tasks such as file manipulation, data processing, and system administration.

DevOps and Configuration Management:

Tools like Chef and Puppet, used for automating infrastructure and server configuration, are written in Ruby. Ruby's readability and ease of use make it a good fit for creating and maintaining configuration management scripts.

Testing Frameworks:

Ruby has robust testing frameworks, including RSpec, Cucumber, and MiniTest. These frameworks are widely used for implementing automated tests and practicing test-driven development (TDD).

API Development:

Ruby is employed in the development of RESTful APIs. Its simplicity and the availability of frameworks like Grape make it a good choice for building APIs.

Data Analysis and Visualization:

Ruby, along with libraries like Numo and Daru, is used for data analysis and manipulation. Visualization tools like Rubyvis and Rubyplot enable developers to create charts and graphs.

Command-Line Tools:

Ruby's ability to handle command-line tasks efficiently makes it suitable for developing command-line tools and utilities.

Content Management Systems (CMS):

Some content management systems, like Radiant CMS, are built using Ruby. These systems provide a flexible and customizable platform for managing digital content.

Desktop Applications:

While not as common as in web development, Ruby can be used for building desktop applications. Shoes is a GUI toolkit for Ruby that facilitates desktop application development.

Education and Learning:

Ruby is often used as a teaching language due to its readability and simplicity. Educational platforms use Ruby to introduce programming concepts to beginners.

Networking Applications:

Ruby's built-in libraries and frameworks, along with its ease of use, make it suitable for developing networking applications, including chat applications and network utilities.

Game Development:

Although not as prevalent as in some other languages, Ruby is used for developing simple games. Libraries like Gosu provide a platform for game development in Ruby.

E-commerce Platforms:

Some e-commerce platforms, including Spree Commerce, are built using Ruby on Rails. These platforms provide a foundation for creating online stores and managing transactions.

Financial Applications:

Ruby is used in the development of financial applications and tools. Its flexibility allows developers to create custom solutions for financial analysis and management.

These applications demonstrate the versatility of Ruby across a range of development tasks and industries. The language's emphasis on developer happiness and productivity continues to attract developers in various domains.

IV
Limitations of RUBY

While Ruby is a powerful and flexible programming language, it has some limitations. Considering these factors is important when deciding whether Ruby is the right choice for a particular project.

Here are some limitations of Ruby:

Performance:

Ruby is often criticized for its performance, especially when compared to languages like C or Java. The Global Interpreter Lock (GIL) in the standard Ruby interpreter (MRI) can hinder parallel execution, limiting performance gains on multi-core systems.

Concurrency:

The GIL also affects concurrency, making it challenging to achieve true parallelism in specific scenarios. While alternative Ruby implementations (like JRuby and Rubinius) address this, the GIL remains a limitation in MRI.

Memory Consumption:

Ruby applications can consume more memory than those written in languages with lower-level memory control. This can be a concern for applications with high memory requirements.

Start-up Time:

The start-up time of Ruby applications, especially in interpreted languages, can be slower compared to compiled languages. This can impact the performance of short-lived scripts or command-line tools.

Mobile Development:

While there are frameworks like RubyMotion for mobile development, Ruby is not as widely used in the mobile development ecosystem as languages like Java (for Android) or Swift (for iOS).

Limited Multithreading:

Although Ruby supports multithreading, the GIL limits the effectiveness of parallel threads, making it less suitable for CPU-bound tasks that require intensive parallel processing.

Learning Curve for Newcomers:

Some beginners find the syntax of Ruby, especially its use of symbols and blocks, a bit challenging to grasp initially. The flexibility and expressiveness that make Ruby powerful can also contribute to a steeper learning curve.

Limited Native Mobile App Support:

Ruby does not have native support for mobile app development compared to languages like Swift (for iOS) or Kotlin/Java (for Android). While there are frameworks like RubyMotion, they are not as widely adopted.

Limited Tooling:

While Ruby has a solid set of development tools, IDE support and specific advanced tools may not be as extensive or mature as those available for some other languages.

Community Size:

While Ruby has a strong and vibrant community, it may not be as large as communities for some other programming languages. This can impact the availability of resources and third-party libraries for niche domains.

Deployment Complexity:

Deploying Ruby applications may be more complex than languages with more standardized deployment processes. Dependency management and versioning can sometimes be challenging.

Less Popular in Certain Industries:

While widely used in web development, Ruby may be less common in specific industries or domains, affecting the availability of specialized expertise or tools.

Despite these limitations, Ruby remains a popular and practical choice for many developers, particularly in web development and other domains where its strengths in expressiveness and developer happiness outweigh these drawbacks. Additionally, ongoing efforts, such as advancements in alternative implementations and the development of Just-In-Time (JIT) compilers, aim to address some of these limitations.

V

Multiple Type Questions With Solutions on RUBY Programming

1. *What is Ruby?*

A. *A precious gemstone*

B. *A programming language*

C. *A database management system*

D. *A graphic design tool*

Solution: B. A programming language

2. Who is the creator of Ruby?

A. Guido van Rossum

B. Yukihiro Matsumoto

C. Larry Wall

D. James Gosling

Solution: B. Yukihiro Matsumoto

3. In Ruby, what is the file extension for a Ruby script?

A. .r

B. .py

C. .rb

D. .ru

Solution: C. .rb

4. Which of the following is used to print output in Ruby?

A. puts

B. print

C. echo

D. display

Solution: A. puts

5. What does the "puts" method do in Ruby?

A. Prints a string with a newline character

B. Prints a string without a newline character

C. *Puts the program to sleep*

D. *Performs mathematical calculations*

Solution: A. *Prints a string with a newline character*

6. *How do you define a variable in Ruby?*

A. *var x;*

B. *$x;*

C. *x = 5;*

D. *define x;*

Solution: C. *x = 5;*

7. *What is the result of 5 + "3" in Ruby?*

A. *8*

B. *"53"*

C. TypeError

D. 15

Solution: C. TypeError

8. What does the "if" statement do in Ruby?

A. Iterates over a collection

B. Defines a method

C. Controls conditional execution

D. Imports a library

Solution: C. Controls conditional execution

9. What is the purpose of the "elsif" keyword in Ruby?

A. Used for iteration

B. Used in regular expressions

C. Adds alternative conditions to an "if" statement

D. Declares a class

Solution: C. Adds alternative conditions to an "if" statement

10. Which symbol is used for single-line comments in Ruby?

- A. # - B. // - C. -- - D. /* */

Solution: A. #

11. What is the purpose of the "each" method in Ruby? -

A. Defines a class - B. Iterates over a collection -

C. Prints output - D. Performs mathematical calculations

Solution: B. Iterates over a collection

12. How do you define a method in Ruby? -

A. def method_name - B. define method_name - C. function method_name - D. method method_name

Solution: A. def method_name

13. What does the term "symbol" represent in Ruby? -

A. A string - B. A numeric value - C. A unique identifier - D. A boolean variable

Solution: C. A unique identifier

14. Which operator is used for exponentiation in Ruby? -

A. ^ - B. ** - C. // - D. %

Solution: B. **

15. What is the purpose of the "case" statement in Ruby? -

A. Defines a class - B. Handles exceptions - C. Controls conditional execution - D. Simplifies multiple "if" statements

Solution: D. Simplifies multiple "if" statements

16. What is the result of the expression "true && false" in Ruby? -

A. true - B. false - C. TypeError - D. nil

Solution: B. false

17. In Ruby, how do you concatenate two strings? -

A. str1 . str2 - B. str1 + str2 - C. str1 : str2 - D. concat(str1, str2)

Solution: B. str1 + str2

18. What is the purpose of the "gets" method in Ruby? -

A. Gets the current time - B. Gets user input from the console - C. Gets a random number - D. Gets the file size

Solution: B. Gets user input from the console

19. How do you define an array in Ruby? -

A. arr = [1, 2, 3] - B. array(1, 2, 3) - C. set = [1, 2, 3] - D. define_array [1, 2, 3]

Solution: A. arr = [1, 2, 3]

20. What is the purpose of the "each_with_index" method in Ruby? -

A. Iterates over a collection with its index - B. Deletes elements from a collection - C. Checks if an element exists in a collection - D. Reverses the order of elements in a collection

Solution: A. Iterates over a collection with its index

21. Which keyword is used to inherit a class in Ruby? -

A. include - B. inherit - C. extends - D. <

Solution: D. <

22. What is the purpose of the "super" keyword in Ruby? -

A. Calls the superclass method - B. Ends the program - C. Defines a new method - D. Skips the current iteration

Solution: A. Calls the superclass method

23. What results from the expression "3.times { |i| puts i }" in Ruby? -

A. 3 - B. 0 1 2 - C. 1 2 3 - D. 0 1 2 3

Solution: B. 0 1 2

24. How do you open and read a file in Ruby? -

A. open_file("filename.txt", "r") - B. File.read("filename.txt") - C. read_file "filename.txt" - D. file_open("filename.txt")

Solution: A. open_file("filename.txt", "r")

25. What is the purpose of the "attr_accessor" in Ruby? -

A. Adds an attribute to a class - B. Accesses elements in an array - C. Creates a new object - D. Provides read and write access to an instance variable

Solution: D. Provides read and write access to an instance variable

26. What is the primary purpose of the "initialize" method in Ruby? -

A. To define instance variables - B. To create a new object - C. To initialize a class variable - D. To end the program

Solution: A. To define instance variables

27. How do you check if a variable is nil in Ruby? -

A. variable.nil? - B. is_nil(variable) - C. variable == null - D. check_nil(variable)

Solution: A. variable.nil?

28. What does the term "RubyGems" refer to in Ruby? -

A. Precious stones in Ruby - B. Built-in Ruby functions - C. Ruby libraries or packages - D. Ruby errors and exceptions

Solution: C. Ruby libraries or packages

29. What is the purpose of the "require" keyword in Ruby? -

A. To define a new class - B. To include a module - C. To load an external file or library - D. To create an instance variable

Solution: C. To load an external file or library

30. How do you define a constant in Ruby? -

A. constant x = 5 - B. x = 5 (constant) - C. CONST = 5 - D. define_constant 5

Solution: C. CONST = 5

31. What does the "yield" keyword do in Ruby? -

A. Terminates the program - B. Calls a block associated with a method - C. Raises an exception - D. Prints output to the console

Solution: B. Calls a block associated with a method

32. What is the purpose of the "module" keyword in Ruby? -

A. To create a class - B. To define a constant - C. To encapsulate methods and constants - D. To end a program execution

Solution: C. To encapsulate methods and constants

33. How do you iterate over a range of numbers in Ruby? -

A. for i in range - B. range.each do |i| - C. iterate range i - D. loop(range)

Solution: B. range.each do |i|

34. What does the term "duck typing" refer to in Ruby? -

A. Typing on a keyboard shaped like a duck - B. Determining an object's type based on its behavior - C.

Using ducks as variable names - D. Typing quacks into the code

Solution: B. Determining an object's type based on its behavior

35. How do you check if a key exists in a hash in Ruby?
-

A. hash.key?(key) - B. key in hash - C. hash.include_key?(key) - D. check_key(hash, key)

Solution: A. hash.key?(key)

36. What is the purpose of the "self" keyword in Ruby?
-

A. Refers to the current class or module - B. Ends the program execution - C. Prints the program output - D. Creates a new instance variable

Solution: A. Refers to the current class or module

37. How do you convert a string to an integer in Ruby?
-

A. *str.to_i* - B. *int(str)* - C. *convert_int(str)* - D. *str.integer*

Solution: A. str.to_i

38. Which method is used to sort an array in Ruby? -

A. array.sort - B. sort_array(array) - C. array.order - D. order_array(array)

Solution: A. array.sort

39. What does the term "DSL" stand for in the context of Ruby? -

A. Domain-Specific Language - B. Dynamic System Language - C. Data Structure Library - D. Detailed Syntax Language

Solution: A. Domain-Specific Language

40. How do you define a class method in Ruby? -

A. def method_name - B. define_class_method method_name - C. self.method_name - D. class_method method_name

Solution: C. self.method_name

41. What is the purpose of the "attr_reader" in Ruby? -

A. Provides write-only access to an instance variable - B. Provides read-only access to an instance variable - C. Provides both read and write access to an instance variable - D. Removes an instance variable from a class

Solution: B. Provides read-only access to an instance variable

42. How do you raise a custom exception in Ruby? -

A. raise_exception("message") - B. exception("message") - C. raise "message" - D. custom_exception("message")

Solution: C. raise "message"

43. Which operator is used for string interpolation in Ruby? -

A. + - B. - - C. * - D. #

Solution: D. #

44. What is the purpose of the "include" keyword in Ruby? -

A. Includes a module in a class - B. Imports a library - C. Adds a constant to a class - D. Includes a file in the program

Solution: A. Includes a module in a class

45. How do you remove an element from the end of an array in Ruby? -

A. array.remove_last - B. array.pop -

C. array.delete_last - D. remove_element(array, -1)

Solution: B. array.pop

46. What is the purpose of the "protected" keyword in Ruby? -

A. Restricts access to methods within the class - B. Provides public access to methods - C. Enables garbage collection - D. Defines a constant

Solution: A. Restricts access to methods within the class

47. How do you convert a symbol to a string in Ruby? -

A. symbol.to_str - B. str(symbol) - C. symbol.to_s - D. convert_str(symbol)

Solution: C. symbol.to_s

48. What does " ORM " mean in Ruby on Rails development? -

A. Object-Relational Model - B. Object-Relational Mapping - C. Object-Rendering Model - D. Object-Rendering Mapping

Solution: B. Object-Relational Mapping

49. *Which method is used to concatenate two arrays in Ruby? -*

A.   *array.concatenate(other_array)*   -   B. *array.concat(other_array) -*

C. *merge_arrays(array, other_array) -* D. *array + other_array*

Solution: B. array.concat(other_array)

50. *How do you define a constant within a module in Ruby? -*

A. *module CONSTANT_NAME - B. const_in_module CONSTANT_NAME - C. module.constant CONSTANT_NAME - D. module ::CONSTANT_NAME*

Solution: D. module ::CONSTANT_NAME

About The Author

Dheeraj Mehrotra, MS, MPhil, PhD (Education Management)., a white and a yellow belt in SIX SIGMA, a Certified NLP Business Diploma holder, is an Educational Innovator, Author, with expertise in Six Sigma In Education, Academic Audits, Neuro-Linguistic Programming (NLP), Total Quality Management In Education, an Experiential Educator, a CBSE Resource towards School Assessment (SQAA), CCE, JIT, Five S, and KAIZEN. He has authored over 100 books on computer science, AI, digital body language, NLP, quality circles, school management, classroom effectiveness, and school safety and security. A former Principal at De Indian Public School, New Delhi, (INDIA), NPS International School, Guwahati, and Education Officer at GEMS, Gurgaon, with ample teaching experience of over Two Decades, he is a certified Trainer for Quality Circles/ TQM in Education and QCI Standards for School Accreditation/ School Audits and Management. He has also been honoured with the President of India's National Teacher Award in 2006 and the Best Science Teacher State Award (By the Ministry of Science and Technology, State of UP), Innovation in Education for his inception of Six Sigma In Education by Education Watch, New Delhi and Education World- Best Teacher Award, BOLT Learner Teacher Award by Air India, 'Innovation in Education Award 2016' by Higher Education Forum (HEF), Gujarat Chapter, among others. He has developed over 150 FREE EDUCATIONAL MOBILE Apps for the Google Play Store exclusively for Teachers, Students, and Parents. This work has been recognised by the LIMCA BOOK OF RECORDS and INDIA BOOK OF RECORDS as the only Indian to draw that feast. Dr Mehrotra is a PRINCIPAL at KUNWARS GLOBAL SCHOOL, Lucknow, India. He has conducted over 1000 workshops globally on "Excellence In Education" integrated with Total Quality Management and Six Sigma, Technology Integration in Education (TIE), Developing towards being ROCKSTAR TEACHERS, including Cyberspace, Cyber

Security, Classroom Management, School Leadership & Management, and Innovative teaching within classrooms via Mind Maps, NLP and Experiential Learning in Academics. He is an active TEDx speaker and can be viewed on the YouTube TEDx channel. As a premium UDEMY Instructor, he has developed over 450 courses and caters to over 8 Lakh students from 180 countries. He can be visited at www.authordheerajmehrotra.com